DISCARD

THE
NBA
A HISTORY OF HOOPS

Published by Creative Education
P.O. Box 227, Mankato, Minnesota 56002
Creative Education is an imprint of The Creative Company
www.thecreativecompany.us

Design and production by Christine Vanderbeek
Art direction by Rita Marshall

Printed by Corporate Graphics in the United States of America

Photographs by Larry Berman, Corbis (Kelly Mooney Photography), Dreamstime
(Munktcu), Getty Images (Nathaniel S. Butler/NBAE, Lou Capozzola/NBAE, Ned
Dishman/NBAE, Sam Forencich/NBAE, Jesse D. Garrabrant/NBAE, Walter Ioss Jr./
Sports Illustrated, Manny Millan/Sports Illustrated, Ronald C. Modra/Sports Imagery,
Layne Murdoch/NBAE, Rich Pilling/NBAE, Dick Raphael/NBAE, Eliot J. Schechter,
Rolf Sjogren, SM/AIUEO, Mike Stobe, Noren Trotman/NBAE, Ron Turenne/NBAE),
iStockphoto (Brandon Laufenberg)

Library of Congress Cataloging-in-Publication Data
Goodman, Michael E.
The story of the New Jersey Nets / by Michael E. Goodman.
p. cm. — (The NBA: a history of hoops)
Includes index.
Summary: The history of the New Jersey Nets professional basketball
team from its start as the New Jersey Americans in 1967 to today,
spotlighting the franchise's best players and most dramatic moments.
ISBN 978-1-58341-953-3
1. New Jersey Nets (Basketball team)—History—Juvenile literature.
I. Title. II. Series.
GV885.32.N37G66 2010   796.323'640974941—dc22   2009035029

CPSIA: 120109 PO1093

First Edition
2 4 6 8 9 7 5 3 1

Page 3: Guard Courtney Lee
Pages 4–5: Guard/forward Vince Carter

THE STORY OF THE
NEW JERSEY NETS

MICHAEL E. GOODMAN

CREATIVE ● EDUCATION

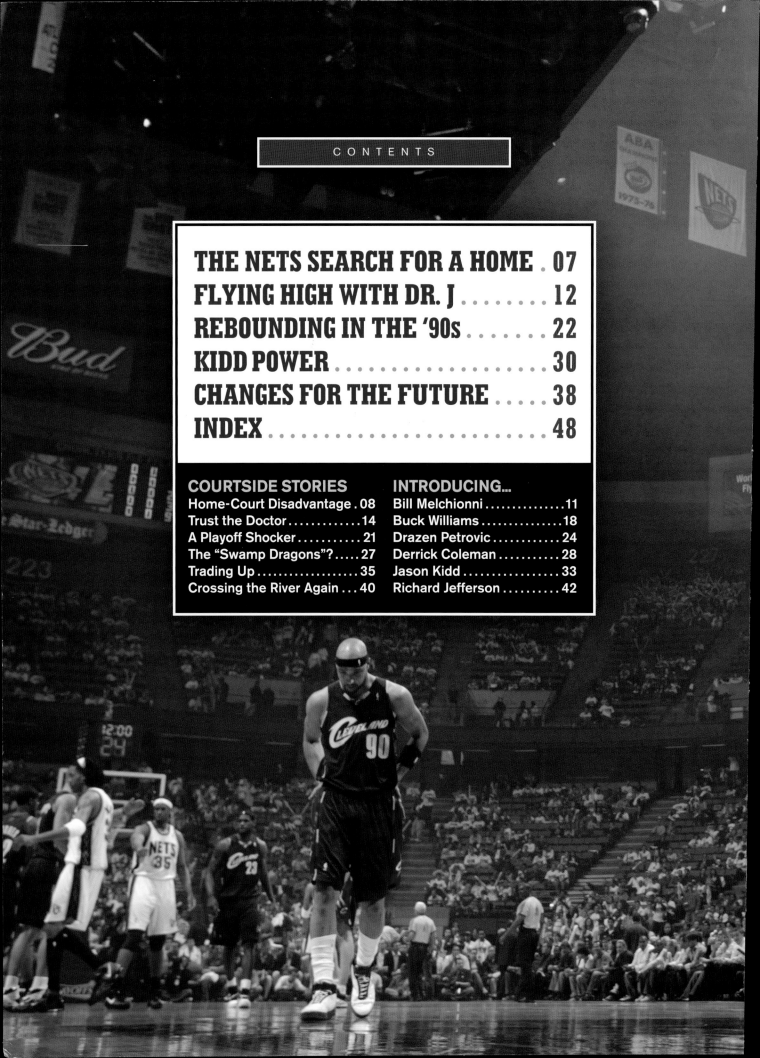

CONTENTS

CHAPTER ONE

THE NETS SEARCH FOR A HOME

The state of New Jersey is famous for many firsts. The first light bulb, phonograph, and motion picture projector were invented in New Jersey by Thomas Edison. The state was the site of the first movie studio in 1893 and the first drive-in movie theater in 1933. The first television for home use was manufactured in New Jersey in 1933, and the first FM radio broadcasts originated in "The Garden State" in 1936.

The state is also proud of its sports firsts. For example, the first baseball game played under organized rules took place in Hoboken in 1846, and the first college football game was an 1869 battle between two New Jersey universities, Princeton and Rutgers. It was not until nearly 100 years later, however, that New Jersey residents were able to cheer for their own professional basketball team. That club, founded in 1967 as the New Jersey Americans and now known as the Nets, has played its games in two different leagues in two different states and has called six arenas home throughout its exciting history.

The Izod Center (formerly called Continental Airlines Arena) in East Rutherford, New Jersey, was the home of the Nets from 1981 to 2010.

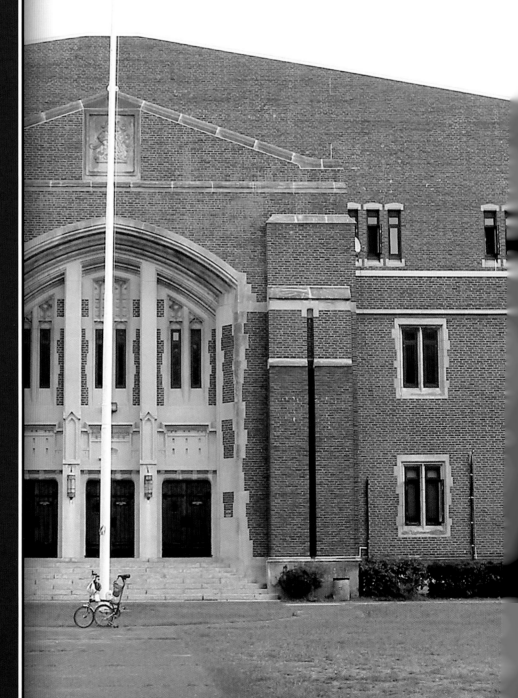

PLAYING IN THE TEANECK ARMORY WAS OFTEN AN ADVENTURE FOR THE NEW JERSEY AMERICANS IN THEIR FIRST SEASON IN THE ABA. Still, the team achieved a respectable 36–42 record, tied with the Kentucky Colonels for fourth place in the Eastern Division. The two clubs were scheduled to face off in New Jersey in a one-game tiebreaker, with the winner earning a playoff berth. However, a circus was booked at the Armory for the selected date, so the Americans had to look for a new "home" court. The only place management could find on short notice was the aging Commack Arena on New York's Long Island. When the two clubs and their fans arrived for the game, they discovered that the arena's floor was missing several boards, and the stands were falling apart. ABA commissioner George Mikan ruled the game a forfeit, and New Jersey was eliminated from the playoffs without taking a single shot. Ironically, the Americans moved the next season to a newly repaired Commack Arena, but their bad luck in the building continued, as they finished with a league-low 17–61 record.

New Jersey's pro basketball team got off to a rocky start as an original member of the American Basketball Association (ABA) in 1967. League officials initially hoped that the team would be based in New York City and challenge the Knicks of the established National Basketball Association (NBA) for fan support. However, the team's owner, Arthur Brown, couldn't find a suitable arena and had to take his club across the Hudson River to play in Teaneck's dark and gloomy Teaneck Armory. Because the building's roof leaked, one home game even had to be postponed due to rain. Led by high-scoring swingman Tony Jackson and center Hank Whitney, the Americans finished their first season 36–42.

The next season, the Americans had a new home and a new name. Brown relocated the club to New York's Long Island and changed its name to the New York Nets to rhyme with two other New York professional sports teams based nearby, baseball's Mets and football's Jets. The Nets suffered through a disappointing 17–61 season, and fewer than 1,000 people showed up to see most of the club's home games. In 1969, a wealthy businessman named Roy Boe bought the team and moved it to a third arena located a little closer to New York City.

Boe made some key moves that increased New York sports fans' interest in the Nets. First, he lured point guard Bill Melchionni from the NBA's Philadelphia 76ers. Melchionni had quick hands and feet, and his

presence soon improved the team's speed and offensive flow. Before the 1970–71 season, Boe hired popular local college coach Lou Carnesecca to take over the reins of the club and engineered a trade for the team's first superstar, forward Rick Barry. Barry had been one of the top scorers in the NBA but jumped leagues because of a contract dispute with his former club, the San Francisco Warriors. "Rick was a scoring machine," said Kentucky Colonels forward Dan Issel, a future Basketball Hall-of-Famer. "I once heard him say that he expected to score 30 points a night. He had it all figured out: he'd take 20 shots, make 12, and then he'd get to the foul line 6 or 8 times to pick up the rest. He talked about it like anyone could do it."

Barry, Melchionni, and center Billy "The Whopper" Paultz helped the Nets post a winning record for the first time in 1971–72. The club even reached the final round of the ABA playoffs that year before losing the championship to the Indiana Pacers.

INTRODUCING...

BILL MELCHIONNI

POSITION GUARD
HEIGHT 6-FOOT-1
NETS SEASONS 1969–76

AS AN ALL-AMERICAN GUARD AT VILLANOVA UNIVERSITY, BILL MELCHIONNI RANKED NINTH IN THE NATION IN SCORING. Then he was drafted by the powerful Philadelphia 76ers, who were led by center Wilt Chamberlain, and he learned to pass first and shoot second. He carried this valuable lesson with him when he switched leagues and joined the Nets in 1969. Melchionni quickly became the glue that held the Nets' offense together. In his first year in New York, Melchionni averaged 15.2 points and 5.7 assists a game. He blossomed the next season, 1970–71, leading the ABA in assists (with a total of 672) while also averaging 17.6 points per game. Melchionni topped the league in assists the next year as well and was also the point man in the Nets' devastating pressing defense. He helped the Nets win ABA championships in 1974 as a player and in 1976 as a player/assistant coach. The 1976 ABA title game was Melchionni's last as a player, but his retired number 25 Nets jersey soon hung proudly from the rafters in the Izod Center at the Meadowlands.

CHAPTER TWO

FLYING HIGH WITH DR. J

The team's prospects suffered a serious blow before the next season when a judge ruled that Barry had to return to the Warriors to complete his contract. Boe soon made up for the loss by trading with the Virginia Squires for highflying Julius Erving, who was nicknamed "Dr. J" for the way he "operated" on the court. The 6-foot-6 forward moved with astonishing speed and grace, and his soaring dunks filled sports highlight films. "Doc goes up and never comes down," said Melchionni.

The Nets didn't come down either during the 1973–74 season, Dr. J's first with the club. They won 55 regular-season games, which was 25 more than their total the previous year. Then the Nets routed the Utah Stars in the league finals to win their first ABA championship, and Dr. J earned his own title—ABA Most Valuable Player (MVP). Two seasons later, the

Arguably the greatest player in the history of the ABA, Dr. J helped take basketball to new levels of excitement with his aerial highlights.

DURING THE NETS' RUN TO THEIR FIRST ABA CHAMPIONSHIP IN 1974, THEY FACED OFF AGAINST THE KENTUCKY COLONELS IN THE SECOND ROUND OF THE PLAYOFFS. The Colonels, led by center Artis Gilmore and forward Dan Issel, always gave the Nets problems. Still, New York won the first two games of the series at home. Game 3 came

down to the final seconds tied 87–87, and Nets coach Kevin Loughery called timeout to set up a last play. Forward Julius Erving laid a hand on the coach's shoulder and said, "Kevin, I'll take the last shot." Loughery nodded and then said, "Okay, guys, but if Doc misses—" Erving cut off the coach again, saying, "Kevin, I won't miss." Erving received the inbounds pass, waited a

few seconds to let the clock run down, and then drove towards his right. He leaped off the wrong foot and banked the shot in from an almost impossible angle for the win. Everyone in the arena was stunned. The Nets completed the series sweep three nights later and then easily captured the ABA Finals for their first league title.

Nets staged a virtual replay of their first championship campaign. They duplicated their 55–29 record, Dr. J again led the league in scoring with an average of 29.3 points per game, and New York romped to its second—and last—ABA title.

The 1975–76 season marked the end of the ABA's brief history, for in the summer of 1976, the ABA and NBA merged, with the Nets and three other ABA franchises joining the older league. But becoming an NBA franchise cost the Nets dearly. The team was required to pay a $3-million entry fee to the NBA and an additional $4.8 million to the Knicks to be allowed to share their region. The financial fallout made it impossible for Dr. J to receive a promised raise, forcing Boe to sell Erving's contract to the Philadelphia 76ers even before Dr. J could play his first NBA game with the Nets. "How could anyone do this to us?" wondered New York guard "Super John" Williamson. "Our season is over already." Williamson turned out to be right. Without the Doctor, the 1976–77 Nets finished at the bottom of the NBA standings with a dismal 22–60 record.

Before the next season, Boe moved the Nets back to their original state, and the New Jersey Nets were officially born in September 1977. The team also acquired a new offensive star—sensational rookie forward Bernard King. During the Nets' first years in New Jersey, the nucleus of King, Williamson, and shot-blocking center George Johnson kept the Nets near the middle of the NBA standings, but the team continued to post losing records. By the 1979–80 season, King and Williamson were traded away as Nets management searched for a winning combination.

Things began to come together in New Jersey two years later when veteran NBA coach Larry Brown took over the team. Brown's first move was to select 21-year-old power forward Buck Williams in the 1981 NBA Draft. A rugged rebounder and scorer, Williams averaged 12.3 boards

NETS

17

INTRODUCING...

BUCK WILLIAMS

POSITION FORWARD
HEIGHT 6-FOOT-8
NETS SEASONS 1981–89

WHEN THE NETS SELECTED BUCK WILLIAMS OUT OF THE UNIVERSITY OF MARYLAND WITH THE THIRD PICK IN THE 1981 NBA DRAFT, THEY KNEW THEY WERE GETTING A HARD-NOSED COMPETITOR AND AN OUTSTANDING PERSON.

Williams spent the first 8 of his 17 NBA seasons in New Jersey and set most of the team's career scoring and rebounding records. As of 2010, he was 1 of only 9 NBA players to have amassed 16,000 points and 13,000 rebounds. At 6-foot-8 and 215 pounds, Williams wasn't the biggest man on the court, but he was one of the strongest. He knew how to establish a dominant rebounding position and also played outstanding defense. Williams earned respect not only for his playing ability but also for his sportsmanship. "I think players have an obligation to the public to carry themselves in a certain way," Williams once said. "I never wanted to do anything to embarrass myself, the organization, or my family. My father always told me that a good name means more than a million dollars." The Nets retired his number 52 jersey in 1999.

and 15.5 points per game to win the NBA Rookie of the Year award. "Every team should be blessed with a Buck Williams," said former Nets star Rick Barry. "He's consistent, hardworking, and tough."

Coach Brown combined Williams with guards Micheal Ray Richardson and Otis Birdsong, "dunk-meister" Darryl Dawkins at center, and sharpshooting forward Albert King (Bernard's younger brother) to create a well-balanced unit. Playing their games in the new Brendan Byrne Arena (later named the Izod Center) in the Meadowlands sports complex in northern New Jersey, the Nets rose among the NBA's elite teams with a 49–33 record in 1982–83, third best in the Eastern Conference's Atlantic Division. Everything was looking up until the last two weeks of the season, when Brown announced that he would be leaving the team to coach at the University of Kansas. Brown's decision seemed to deflate the young Nets, who quickly shuffled out of the playoffs.

The team stayed above .500 for two more seasons under new coach Stan Albeck and even pulled off a major upset by eliminating Julius Erving's 76ers in an exciting first-round matchup in the 1984 playoffs. Then the Nets went on an extended drought for the rest of the 1980s, reaching their low point when they assembled a franchise-worst 17–65 record in 1989–90.

Micheal Ray Richardson was a slick passer and dangerous scorer but an even better defender, leading the NBA in steals in four seasons.

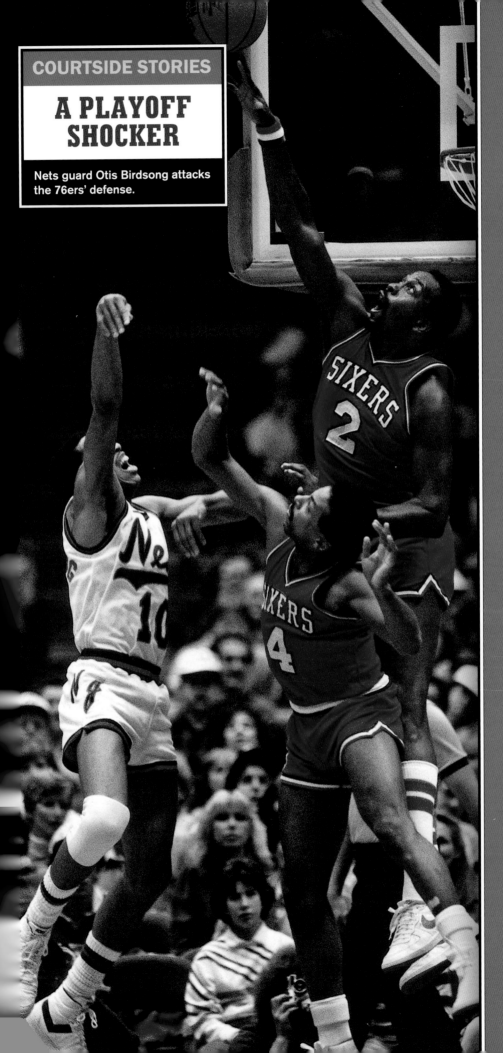

A PLAYOFF SHOCKER

Nets guard Otis Birdsong attacks the 76ers' defense.

BEFORE THE 1984 PLAYOFFS, THE NETS HAD QUALIFIED FOR THE NBA POSTSEASON THREE TIMES BUT HAD YET TO WIN A SINGLE PLAYOFF GAME. Their chances didn't look good in 1984, either, as they would be facing the defending NBA champion Philadelphia 76ers, led by former Nets star Julius Erving. New Jersey shocked the 76ers and most basketball experts by taking the first two games of the series in Philadelphia. Then they headed home looking for a series sweep. But Erving and guard Maurice Cheeks took over, leading Philly to consecutive wins in the Meadowlands and setting up a deciding Game 5 showdown in Philadelphia. Erving assured reporters that the Nets would not win a third time in Philadelphia. "You can mail in the stats," he proclaimed. Erving's prediction looked solid as Philly took a seven-point lead into the closing minutes of the contest. Then guard Micheal Ray Richardson and forward Albert King led a Nets charge that resulted in a thrilling 101–98 victory. The Nets franchise would suffer through the rest of the 1980s, but for one night, the team was a big winner.

CHAPTER THREE

REBOUNDING IN THE '90s

During the Nets' down years, team management committed several blunders in the NBA Draft. First-round picks such as guard Dwayne "Pearl" Washington and forward Chris Morris, who were stars in college, turned out to be busts in the pros. Then, under new coach Bill Fitch, the club made two outstanding draft picks in the early 1990s—power forward Derrick Coleman and point guard Kenny Anderson. Talented but moody, Coleman could dominate games when he was motivated, hitting 18-foot jumpers with deadly accuracy or making daring moves inside. Anderson was an outstanding passer and penetrator, but, like Coleman, he could be inconsistent.

This talented duo, along with long-range bomber Drazen Petrovic from Croatia—the NBA's first European star—powered the Nets to a 43–39 record in 1992–93, ending a seven-year streak of losing seasons. Then, in the summer of 1993, Petrovic was tragically killed in a car accident in Europe when he was there for an off-season tournament. Basketball fans

Never achieving the superstardom that many fans expected, Kenny Anderson would play for eight other NBA teams after leaving the Nets.

PERHAPS THE BEST WORDS TO DESCRIBE DRAZEN PETROVIC WERE "HIGH ENERGY." Chuck Daly, who coached Petrovic in his final Nets season, called him "indefatigable" because he never seemed to get tired. He was a whirlwind on the court and one of the best long-range shooters in NBA history. Petrovic grew up in a small city in Croatia near the Adriatic Sea. There, he practiced for hours every day before and after school, putting up as many as 1,000 shots from all over the court. At age 15, he was named to the Yugoslavian national team and four years later was playing professionally in Spain. By age 25, he was in America as a member of the Portland Trail Blazers and then joined the Nets during the 1990–91 season. "Petro" quickly established himself as one of the league's top three-point shooters. A true pioneer, Petrovic's success in the NBA laid the groundwork for other European stars to come and play in the United States. Almost a decade after his tragic death in 1993, Petrovic was elected to the Basketball Hall of Fame in 2002.

on both sides of the Atlantic Ocean mourned his death. "It's hard for you to imagine here in America, because you have so many great players," Drazen's brother, Aleksander, said. "But we are a country of four million. Without him, basketball [in Croatia] takes three steps back."

Without Petrovic, the Nets and their fans experienced a bittersweet season in 1993–94. The club achieved its second straight winning record (45–37), and both Coleman and Anderson were selected to play in the All-Star Game. But New Jersey was quickly eliminated in the first round of the playoffs by the rival Knicks. Beset by injuries the next year, the Nets fell below .500 again, and team management decided to clean house. Coleman and Anderson were traded during the 1995–96 season, and more deals followed. New arrivals included guard Kendall Gill, swingman Reggie Williams, and 7-foot-6 center Shawn Bradley. Nets fans needed a scorecard to figure out just who was on the floor for their team.

The wheeling and dealing continued into the 1997 NBA Draft when New Jersey sent several players and its first-round pick to Philadelphia for the rights to All-American forward Keith Van Horn, the second pick in the draft. Long and lean, Van Horn was a small forward in a power forward's body. "North to south, up and down the court, he's the fastest big man in the country," said Utah Jazz president Frank Layden. Along with his speed,

DESPITE THE TEAM'S IMPROVE-MENT IN THE EARLY 1990S, THE NETS STILL HAD TROUBLE AT-TRACTING FANS TO THEIR ARENA IN THE MEADOWLANDS. In contrast, the New Jersey Devils hockey team usually played to packed houses in the same arena. So Nets management decided that their club needed a new, livelier image. One marketing executive suggested that a name as catchy as "Devils" might excite fans. He proposed calling the team the "New Jersey Swamp Dragons." The name had a double meaning. Since the site of the Meadowlands had originally been a swamp, it would be historically fitting. More important for marketing purposes, though, was that swamp dragons were loveable pets in a series of popular graphic novels called *Discworld*. The marketing executive envisioned a colorful new logo, based on the graphic novel illustrations, which might excite young fans and prompt them to buy more team merchandise. The team proposed the new name to the NBA's executive committee, where it was rejected by a close vote. The club explored a few other names but decided to stick with "Nets" in the end.

DERRICK COLEMAN HAD THE BODY AND SKILLS TO BE AN NBA GREAT. But it seemed he never wanted to work hard enough to become a real star. A first-team All-American out of Syracuse University, Coleman was the first overall pick in the 1990 NBA Draft. The Nets obtained a forceful rebounder with a soft touch from the outside who was also an excellent passer for a big man. During his five seasons in New Jersey, "D.C." averaged 19.9 points, 10.6 rebounds, and 3.1 assists per game. Such numbers were good enough to earn him NBA Rookie of the Year honors in 1991 and selection as a league All-Star in 1994. But New Jersey coaches also had to deal with Coleman's poor attitude and occasional laziness, and a contract dispute led the Nets to trade him after the 1994–95 season. While Coleman didn't live up to his basketball potential, he did achieve several other lifetime goals. Following retirement, he used his basketball earnings to build a strip mall in his hometown of Detroit, Michigan, and helped revitalize the neighborhood in which he had grown up.

INTRODUCING...

DERRICK COLEMAN

POSITION FORWARD
HEIGHT 6-FOOT-10
NETS SEASONS 1990–95

Van Horn displayed intensity on the boards and possessed an excellent outside shot. He combined with second-year guard Kerry Kittles and power forward Jayson Williams to key an explosive offense that led the Nets back to the playoffs.

The team's revival was short-lived, however, and New Jersey sank quickly to the bottom of the Atlantic Division for the next three years. In an effort to turn things around during the 1998–99 season, the Nets pulled off a blockbuster midseason trade with the Minnesota Timberwolves, obtaining high-scoring point guard Stephon Marbury. Marbury's presence greatly improved the team's offense, but he was a defensive liability. Ironically, Marbury hindered the club's defense in another way when he collided with Williams, the club's best shot-blocker and rebounder, under the New Jersey basket in a late-season contest. Williams suffered a severely broken leg that ended his career.

KIDD POWER

As the new millennium began, the Nets reached back to their ABA days to hire Rod Thorn as team president. Thorn had been a Nets assistant coach when the team won its first ABA championship in 1974. He had later earned a reputation as an astute basketball executive when, as general manager of the Chicago Bulls, he had drafted star guard Michael Jordan. Thorn was now determined to build a strong foundation in New Jersey. His first move was to select forward Kenyon Martin with the top overall pick in the 2000 NBA Draft. Martin loved to battle around the basket for rebounds and emphasized defense before offense. To prove the point, Martin chose six as his uniform number in honor of Bill Russell, one of the best defenders in NBA history.

Thorn's next moves truly turned things around in New Jersey. He hired former Los Angeles Lakers All-Star guard Byron Scott to coach the Nets and made a draft-day trade to bring in rookie small forward Richard Jefferson, whose slashing drives to the basket provided a new dimension to the team's offense. Thorn then engineered a high-level trade of All-Stars with the

Kenyon Martin came into the NBA with big expectations, having just earned college basketball's 2000 National Player of the Year award.

Phoenix Suns in July 2001, sending Marbury out West in exchange for point guard Jason Kidd, one of the NBA's all-time greatest passers. Kidd was more than just an outstanding individual player; his presence improved the whole team. Danny Ainge, a basketball analyst who had once coached Kidd, described his impact on the Nets. "This team has taken on Jason's soul," said Ainge. "Some guys show up to play; some guys show up to win. But the way Jason plays, he elevates everyone else's game because they go, 'My gosh, look at how hard he plays, look how confident he is, look at how tough-minded he is.' It's contagious for the rest of them. They see how hard you have to play to win."

Following Kidd's lead, New Jersey pulled off a 26-game turnaround, going 52–30 and, incredibly, making it all the way to the 2002 NBA Finals. There, the team's championship dreams were quickly crushed by the powerful Los Angeles Lakers, who were led by center Shaquille O'Neal and guard Kobe Bryant. However, the Nets landed on their feet the following season, topping the Atlantic Division once

INTRODUCING...

JASON KIDD

POSITION GUARD
HEIGHT 6-FOOT-4
NETS SEASONS 2001–08

FOR NEW JERSEY NETS FANS, JULY 18, 2001, WAS ONE OF THE MOST SIGNIFICANT DAYS IN TEAM HISTORY. That's when Jason Kidd was traded to the Nets from the Phoenix Suns. Kidd had only average speed and a below-average outside shot, but he possessed the special skills and confidence needed to transform a group of individual players into a winning team. Nets coach Byron Scott was thrilled to have Kidd join his club. "He's a one-man fast break who's quicker with the ball than most NBA players are without it, plus he's a devastating on-the-ball defender and an excellent rebounder," said Scott. "He pushes the ball up, gets us into the open floor, and creates easy shot after easy shot. That's what winning basketball is all about at this level." It was no coincidence that the Nets became the top team in the Eastern Conference once Kidd arrived in New Jersey. During his six and a half seasons with the Nets, the club won nearly 57 percent of its games. A nine-time All-Star, Kidd ranked third in league history in assists and seventh in steals as of 2010.

more and winning 12 of their first 14 playoff games to reach the NBA Finals again. This time, they faced off against the San Antonio Spurs and star center/forward Tim Duncan. The clubs split the first four games, and then San Antonio swept the final two contests to claim the championship.

With two straight Finals appearances under their belt, the Nets and their fans were confident that an NBA title would soon be in their grasp. Then a rift between Kidd and Coach Scott led Thorn to fire Scott during the next season and replace him with assistant coach Lawrence Frank. Frank's high-energy style helped to revitalize the squad, and the Nets won 14 straight games on the way to their third consecutive Atlantic Division title. It was clear that some of the team's magic was beginning to fade, though, when New Jersey was eliminated in the second round of the playoffs.

Roster turmoil and injuries to key team members plagued the Nets in 2004–05. Martin and Kittles left town via trades. Then both Kidd and Jefferson spent part of the year on injured reserve. The team seemed doomed until New Jersey traded with the Toronto Raptors for skywalking swingman Vince Carter. Carter's athletic dunks and long-range shooting thrilled New Jersey fans. He gave the club an amazing new offensive weapon, and once Kidd and Jefferson returned to the lineup, the Nets were ready to soar. The club won 16 of its last 21 games to slip into the playoffs with a 42–40 record, only to be swept in the first round by the Miami Heat.

Pages 36–37: Point guard Jason Kidd dishes to forward Brian Scalabrine.

TRADING UP

Vince Carter elevates for a slam.

TRADES ARE A WAY OF LIFE IN THE NBA, BUT IT LONG SEEMED TO NETS FANS THAT THEY WERE GETTING THE RAW END OF THE DEAL TOO OFTEN. After all, their team had traded away Dr. J (for money) in 1976 as well as other team favorites over the years, such as forwards Buck Williams and Bernard King and guard Kenny Anderson. In 2001, however, Nets management made several trades that all had positive results. In June, they engineered a draft-day swap with the Houston Rockets to obtain forward Richard Jefferson and center Jason Collins. A month later, they exchanged point guards with Phoenix, sending high-scoring Stephon Marbury to the Suns for Jason Kidd, the league's best floor general. Kidd's presence in New Jersey sparked the team to the NBA Finals in both 2002 and 2003. Then, just as it seemed the Nets were poised to trade Kidd in 2004–05, they didn't. Instead, they made a deal with the Raptors for highflying swingman Vince Carter, whose dramatic dunks thrilled fans and lifted the club's offense to new heights.

CHAPTER FIVE

CHANGES
FOR THE FUTURE

Heading into 2005–06, the Nets faced some major deci-
sions both on and off the court. A new ownership group
that had taken over the club in 2004 was eager to move
it back across the Hudson River to the borough of Brooklyn,
but the group encountered obstacles in obtaining permission
to build a new arena. Meanwhile, the Devils hockey team was
preparing to move from the Meadowlands to a new building
in Newark, New Jersey, and hoped the Nets would join them
there. The unsettled situation upset many fans, and the Nets
often played to small crowds at home.

Early in the season, the team seemed headed toward its
first losing record in five years until the Nets' "Three-Headed
Monster" of Kidd, Jefferson, and Carter finally found its groove
in early March. The club finished the year on a high note, cap-
turing its fourth division title in five years and roaring into the
playoffs. After eliminating the Indiana Pacers in the opening
round, the Nets confronted the NBA's hottest team, the Heat,

Although never much of a scorer, seven-foot center Jason Collins gave
the Nets valuable inside muscle for six and a half seasons.

IN AUGUST 2004, AN INVESTOR GROUP LED BY BUSINESSMAN BRUCE RATNER PURCHASED THE NETS. Other owners included hip-hop musician Jay-Z and mystery novelist Mary Higgins Clark. Soon afterwards, Ratner announced his intention to move the club back across the Hudson River and into a proposed new arena to be built in Brooklyn, believing the Nets could fare much better financially in New York than in New Jersey. Some of the Nets' oldest fans, those who had cheered the club in its ABA days as the New York Nets, were thrilled that the team might be moving close to them again. Yet Ratner's plans were stalled by problems in obtaining funding for the new arena or getting permission to build it on land that had been promised by New York City for other purposes. To save money, Ratner prompted management to trade several of the team's highest-priced players—such as guard Kerry Kittles and forwards Kenyon Martin and Richard Jefferson—for players with less expensive or shorter-term contracts. The team took on a new look, and in 2010, work finally began on a new arena in Brooklyn.

COURTSIDE STORIES

CROSSING THE RIVER AGAIN

A view of New York City, across the Hudson River from Jersey City.

who were led by guard Dwyane Wade and center Shaquille O'Neal. The Heat crushed New Jersey in five games on their way to an NBA championship.

The 2006–07 season featured several of the loftiest achievements in team history. The Nets reached the playoffs for the sixth straight time, Kidd was named to the league's All-Defensive team for the fifth time in six years in New Jersey, Carter set a franchise NBA scoring record for points in a season (2,070) and points per game (27.5), and Lawrence Frank became the winningest NBA coach in club history. Yet the Nets finished the season with a mediocre 41–41 record and were again bounced in the second round of the postseason.

RICHARD JEFFERSON

RICHARD JEFFERSON'S ROAD TO STARDOM WITH THE NETS TOOK SOME UNUSUAL TURNS. For one thing, the Nets didn't even select him during the 2001 NBA Draft. They picked Eddie Griffin, a player who had better individual skills than "R. J." but who was not as much of a team player. So the Nets engineered a trade, sending Griffin to the Rockets for Jefferson and center Jason Collins. Once in New Jersey, Jefferson was given a role as backup to forward Keith Van Horn. But he quickly showed that his speed and leaping ability fit better with the up-tempo style the Nets began employing after point guard Jason Kidd joined the team. Van Horn was traded away, and Jefferson became a starter. He played for seven years in New Jersey and left the team in 2008 as its second-leading all-time scorer and ninth-leading all-time rebounder. A humble and generous man, Jefferson donated more than $3.5 million to his alma mater, the University of Arizona, to help finance the construction of a new gymnasium at the school.

R od Thorn knew that it was time for a major shakeup in New Jersey. So did Jason Kidd. The player whose arrival in New Jersey had turned around the franchise requested a trade to a championship contender. Thorn granted Kidd's wish by sending him to the Dallas Mavericks in exchange for guard Devin Harris, whose speed and ball-handling skills reminded some fans of a young Kidd.

In 2007–08, Harris went from being a role player with the Mavericks to becoming lead engineer of the Nets' offense. "It's one heck of a challenge," said Coach Frank. "He's playing the hardest position, coming to a brand-new team, trying to get a feel not only for [his] game but for the four other guys on the court at the time. It's a big-time challenge, but he's really making good progress."

Lawrence Frank (below) coached Devin Harris (opposite) only briefly; 2008–09 was Harris's first full season in New Jersey and Frank's last.

Still, it took a while for the team to adjust to its new point guard, and the Nets missed the 2008 playoffs. At season's end, the team made several other changes in efforts to improve its stock of speedy athletes while reducing payroll costs. Jefferson was traded to the Milwaukee Bucks for athletic Chinese forward Yi Jianlian and veteran small forward Bobby Simmons. Then, in the 2008 NBA Draft, the Nets selected center Brook Lopez and forward Ryan Anderson.

The once-aging Nets were now much younger, taller, and more aggressive. They were also very inexperienced, and it showed. In 2009–10, New Jersey's youthful lineup lost its first 18 games, costing Coach Frank his job. Only a minor surge at the end of the season carried the Nets to a 12–70 finish, keeping them from setting a new NBA record for most losses. "It was an abysmal season," Harris summed up.

Despite their recent struggles, the Nets hope to soon revive their highflying attack and remind fans that they are capable of achieving the same type of success experienced during the Dr. J era and the club's glory days in the ABA. New Jersey's most loyal fans have no doubt that such a turnaround is coming, and they are patiently waiting until the team brings home that elusive first NBA championship trophy.

A seven-footer with unusual speed and quickness, Brook Lopez was one of few bright spots during the Nets' forgettable 2009–10 season.

INDEX